BY MARKY MARK AND LYNN GOLDSMITH

First published in the UK 1992 by BOXTREE LIMITED, Broadwall House, 21 Broadwall, London SE1 9PL

First published in the USA 1992 by HarperPerennial, a division of HarperCollins Publishers, 10 East 53rd Street, New York, N.Y. 10022

1 3 5 7 9 10 8 6 4 2

Designed by Elizabeth Van Itallie

1-85283-880-9

A catalogue record for this book is available from the British Library

Printed and bound in Great Britain by Butler & Tanner Ltd, Frome and London

I wanna dedicate this book to my dick.

BY MARKY MARK AND LYNN GOLDSMITH

MARKY

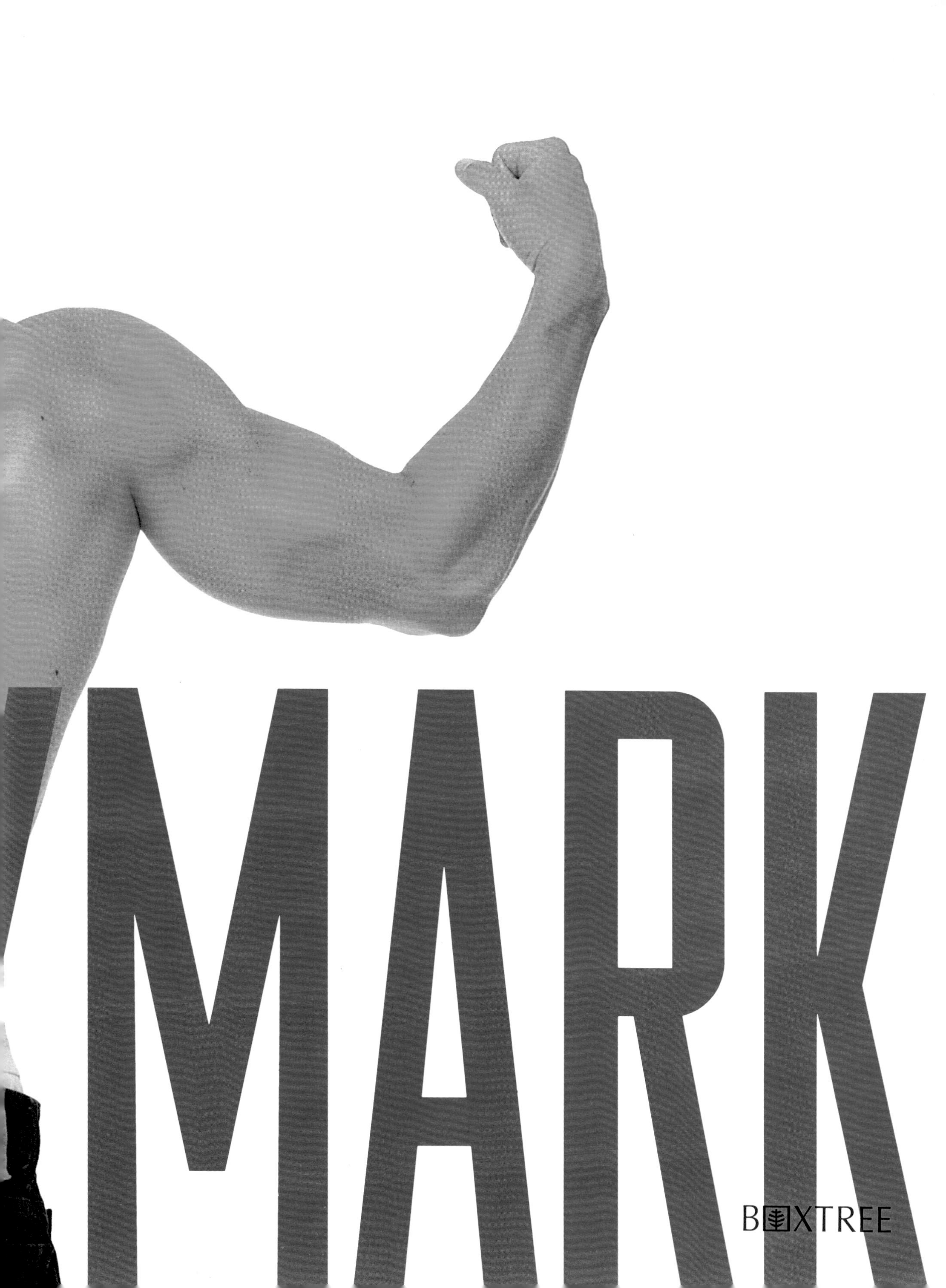
MARK
BOXTREE

WHO IS MARKY

He's someone I met four years ago. Back then he was Mark Wahlberg, "Donnie's little brother." He'd come out on the road with New Kids to hang with Donnie or to cruise girls. He was kinda shy and very respectful to people. I liked him. When Donnie started playing me the music he was working on with Mark, I knew he was going to be "large." I wondered how Alma, their mother, would be able to handle having twice as many girls hanging around outside their home. What I didn't know was how many guys would be into Mark as well. I think he attracted both sexes because he came from the streets and has a very strong physical image. He didn't always have that body. I remember him at 19 as a sorta skinny kid. Mark truly built himself up with hard work and discipline. He takes a lot of pride in the fact that he made a commitment to developing his body and isn't the type of person to choose the easy way.

The first time I saw Mark perform was opening one of the New Kids shows. There was

MARK?

no record, much less a record deal at the time. Mark went out there on stage in front of 40,000 people

and turned it out. I remember looking at Tracey, his sister, and Donnie together on the side of the stage. They were beaming. Shy Mark became rap exhibitionist extraordinaire Marky Mark.

After the album was released I went with Mark and Donnie to a performance he was doing at New York's Ritz. This was the first show where the audience had come just to see Marky Mark and the Funky Bunch. I will never forget it because after the last number me, Mark, Donnie and Robo jumped into the limo for a fast getaway, à la New Kids.

Girls threw themselves all over the car. We were forced to a stop. Mark lowered his window. Hands, arms, mouths and heads came pouring through. Voices screamed out... "Mark I love you." Used to seeing this happen to his brother, he couldn't believe it was for him. In ecstasy he repeated, "Cheese, it's for me, they want me..." Donnie smiled. Yes Mark, they want you. – Lynn Goldsmith

MARK WAS THE **BABY** IN THE FAMILY, AND BABIES HAVE A LOT OF **POWER.** – DONNIE

DO YOU THINK YOU'VE CHANGED IN THE LAST YEAR?

FUCK
YEAH.
MY WHOLE
LIFE HAS
MADE A
FUCKIN'
360° TURN.

RAIDERS

THE FUNKY BUNCH

came before Marky Mark because I already had that name for a group. I thought about doing something with Mark and I didn't want him to be by himself on stage as a white dude rapping. I wanted to fill it up with a lot of activity. And I didn't want it to look like anybody else. – Donnie

My favorite part of the show is "Good Vibrations" because that's the party jam. Everybody likes that song and at the end we take a bow and that's my favorite part because we all hold hands. It's like one big squad at the end. And the band is one really, really slamming band. Donnie put that band together. – Scottie Gee

ROOTS
CANAD
XL

Hector, he's into philosophy. He's always evaluating everything and studying and shit. And always likes to debate upon things. Between him, me, and Boom we always have a deep conversation about politics or religion or something like that.

DJ Terry is like the class clown, he's always getting into some ill shit. Crazy mother-fucker. He loves to fuck. He's always out trying to make a porno movie.

Scottie Gee— he tries to be the pretty boy of the crew. I call him Leather Face, because his face looks like it's made out of leather. He looks like that guy from Texas Chainsaw Massacre.

BEFORE-SHOW PRAYER

Dear Lord, we come to you tonight asking for your guidance, your strength, and your good will. Thank you for helping us all out, helping us to succeed in life. And for giving our family, friends and loved ones your blessings. Deliver us to them safely. I will always pray in your name, and the name of The Father, The Son, and The Holy Spirit. Amen. Let's do it y'all.

MARKY
MARK

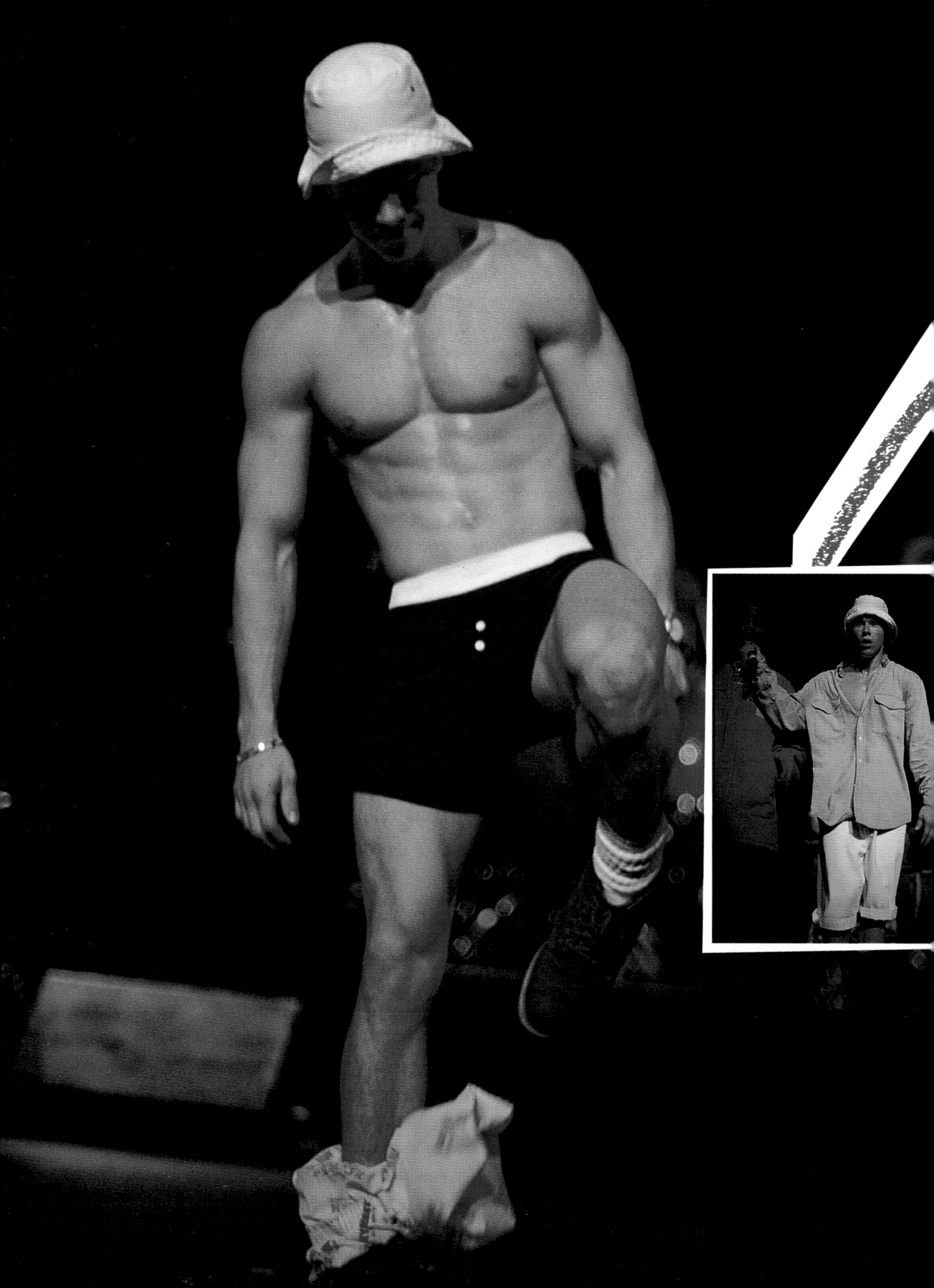

People see him as a white ver-

sion of LL Cool J. – Scottie Gee

The first time I saw Mark on stage I cried. He was opening up for the New Kids and I was terrified for him. I thought that although he seemed confident, deep down he was really afraid. When I went into his dressing room and said "Oh Mark, I'm so afraid for you," he said to me, "What are you so worried about? What's the big deal?" I thought he was going to freak out with stage fright, but he didn't. He came out and was incredible. He was the opposite of

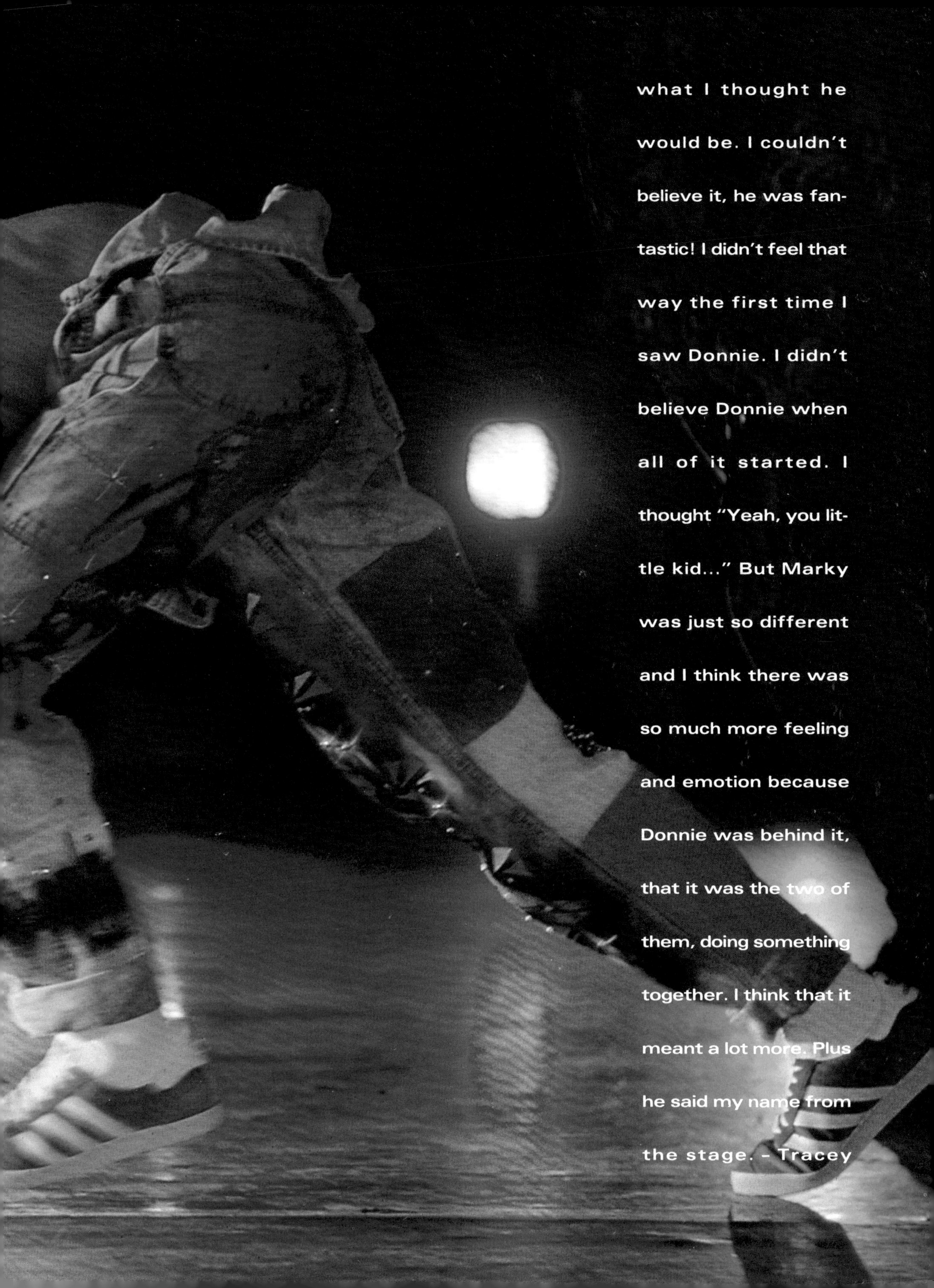

what I thought he would be. I couldn't believe it, he was fantastic! I didn't feel that way the first time I saw Donnie. I didn't believe Donnie when all of it started. I thought "Yeah, you little kid..." But Marky was just so different and I think there was so much more feeling and emotion because Donnie was behind it, that it was the two of them, doing something together. I think that it meant a lot more. Plus he said my name from the stage. – Tracey

SO
YOU'VE
BEEN ON
THE
ROAD
FOR THE
FIRST
TIME-
WHAT
DO YOU
THINK

?

IT'S
DOPE.
IT'S
DOPE.

We were performing in Oslo, Norway. We were on a barge, there were boats all around, and fish, and the water looked really nasty. During the show he kept on looking at the water and then at me. I kept on shaking my head no and then I shook my head yeah just cause I was tired of shaking it no, and I couldn't believe it, he ran and leaped off the barge. It was during the show! It made me think... what's wrong with him? What's wrong with me? – Miguel

Sex

& Hip Hop

WHAT DO YOU FEEL WHEN YOU COME OFFSTAGE?

MARK: TIRED
SCOTTIE: TIRED
TERRY: EXHAUSTED
HECTOR: RELIEVED

Do you like being on the road? Yeah, It's cool,

it's better than staying home. – Scottie Gee

I think people see Marky Mark and The Funky Bunch as this cute phenomenon with a nice body, and some guys doing a cou-

ple of flips. I don't think they really see how much we're all into what we're doing. This is our life and we really enjoy doing this. It's not just some guys showing our muscles. We started putting a good show on but I think a lot of the young girls out there just have an infatuation with Mark looking good and are not really into his lyrics or what he's saying or what we're doing. It's a lot of that. – Hector

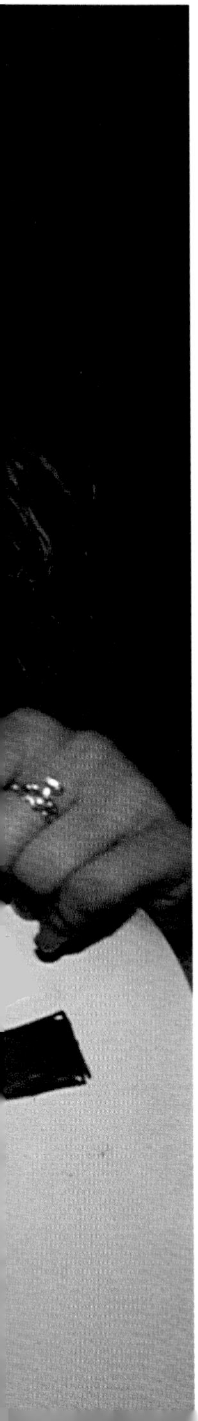

FUNKY BUNCH TRIES TO BE ITS OWN SELF-ESTABLISHED LITTLE GROUP. IT'S LIKE TWO ACTS IN ONE. BUT YEAH, WE MORE OR LESS GET GIRLS NOW SINCE MARK PUT US ON THE MAP WITH HIM. THAT'S MOSTLY WHAT I'M GRATEFUL FOR. – SCOTTIE GEE

The magazines started getting better responses when they put the *whole group* in. Because they were tired of just seeing the same old pictures of Mark. They wanted new flesh. But don't you think a big part of that's also because Mark is a perfect little white teen idol? Yeah, exactly. I don't think they wanted to corrupt that image by putting in three black people, you know what I mean? It was going to cause a lot of conflict and I think the record company was scared, I think everyone was scared, that we would bring him down. There's probably still people blaming us for him not being more successful or whatever. Because we were not being put in the white magazines because we were black, and we weren't being put in the black magazines because Mark was white, you know what I'm saying? There was a whole thing like that. – DJ Terry

HORNETS

THERE'S BEEN TIMES WHEN EACH ONE OF US LEFT THE GROUP. LIKE SCOTT GOT ARGUING WITH MARK, AND LEFT, AND THEN CAME BACK. THEN A COUPLE OF WEEKS LATER I QUIT, AND CAME BACK. AND THEN TERRY QUIT AND CAME BACK. THAT STICKS OUT IN MY MIND A LOT, THOSE TIMES. IT'S LIKE BROTHERS FIGHTING. WE ARGUE AND COME BACK AND BE BROTHERS AGAIN. – HECTOR

The only three best friends that you really have are in the group because they're going through the same things you're going through day in and day out. – DJ Terry

I must say that Donnie Wahlberg is a creator. That's someone you can idolize. He just thinks quick. Mark has a lot to thank him for too, you know

what I'm saying? Cause it could have easily been Donnie Don And The Funky Bunch. It just happens. Life is luck, tell you that right now. – Scottie Gee

A lot of songs on the record I could have easily done for myself. In a way I *did* do them for myself by writing and producing them. Even though the stuff is coming through a different artist, it's still something I'm expressing. It's like if Eric Clapton writes a song for Sting, not to compare me and Marky to them, then Eric Clapton is still expressing himself through the song that Sting is performing. And Sting at the the same time has to find what it is in the song that relates to him, why he expresses it. Marky can't do the songs that I write without finding something in them that is him. But then again I'm expressing myself through him at the same time. ★ When I pick up a magazine and they review his album and there's a smart remark about me and high praise for him like "Oh Marky's nothing like his brother, he's totally different. He is going against the grain that his brother goes in. His lyrics and his music are something Donnie Wahlberg is not in tune with." Obviously those people don't know what they're talking about because they've never read the credits for the album and seen that I wrote the music, arranged the music, and produced the music. I'm sure they don't have a clue as to my involvement in the project, how much energy and thought I put into it, how much time I spent on it. For me to start trying to fight that, to fight people's ignorance, is only going to hurt me and Marky. It won't prove nothin' to them. People believe what they want to believe, and people don't want to believe that I had as much involvement in Marky's stuff as I did. ★ When it comes time for the album to come out and the project has been mostly me and my time, I have to let it go and understand that the success of the album, although I may not get all the credit, is also a success for me. It shows that the vision I set out to make a reality became a reality, and the belief that I had in myself to make it become a reality was correct. I know I can succeed in making my visions come true, and it gives me confidence to try to do it again and again. – Donnie

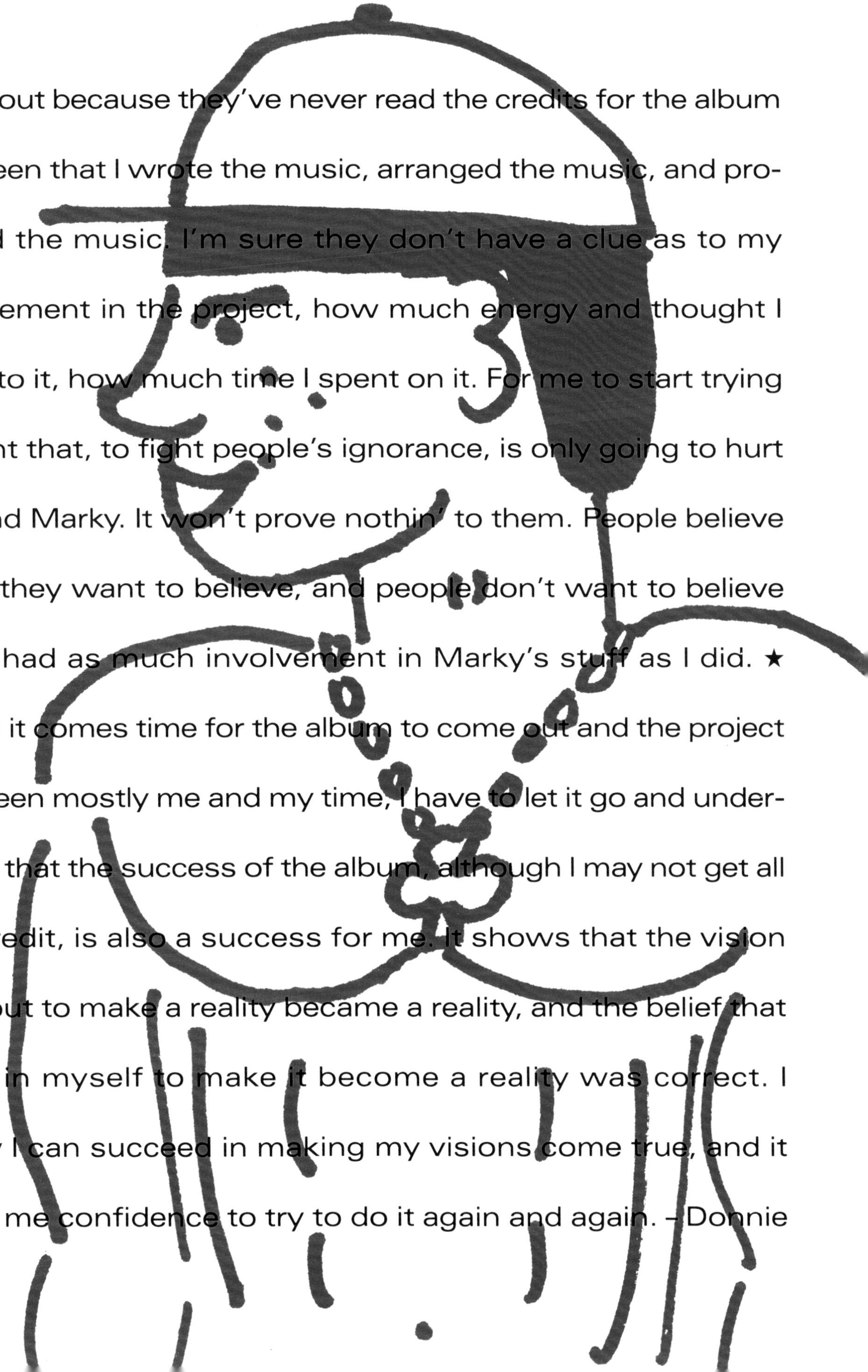

THE WORST THING

you could ever do to an artist that you work with is get caught up in the belief that your role is more important. I can't be Marky Mark in the videos and I'm not Marky Mark on tour bustin' my ass every night. – Donnie

BEFORE he went on, I told him some things to do on stage. He did everything I asked and it worked. He also did about ten things on his own that I didn't tell him to do, and all ten of them worked.

– Donnie

Donnie: Mark was doing a show at Magic Mountain in California. The crowd was about fifty percent girls and fifty percent Mexican kids who came to see the other rap group on the bill. They were starting to compete with the girls who were there to see Marky. We were trying to think of what he could do to get the guys on his side. When he came out, he dropped his pants. It was hilarious. I couldn't stop laughing. He started dancing around the stage... It was funny to see my little brother on stage in his drawers. I didn't think he should keep doing it, but it was so funny that I couldn't tell him to stop. I kept wanting to see him

DO IT AGAIN!

X

The only time I was ever jealous of him was when he told me he went out with a girl who I thought was amazing and he told me she *was* amazing. – Donnie

WELL, THE GIRLS

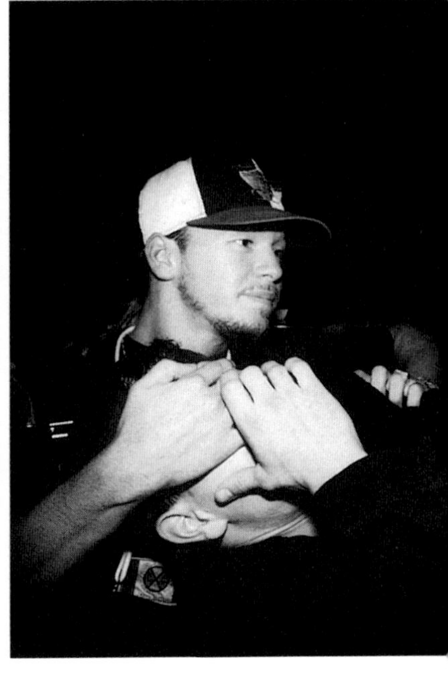

because he's Donnie's brother. That was the main factor. "Oh, he's Donnie's little brother...he's so cute." They more or less thought that Mark was

ALWAYS LIKED HIM

one of those cute youngsters, but as he built his physique he attracted a different crowd. I think he has sex appeal for the women now. – Scottie Gee

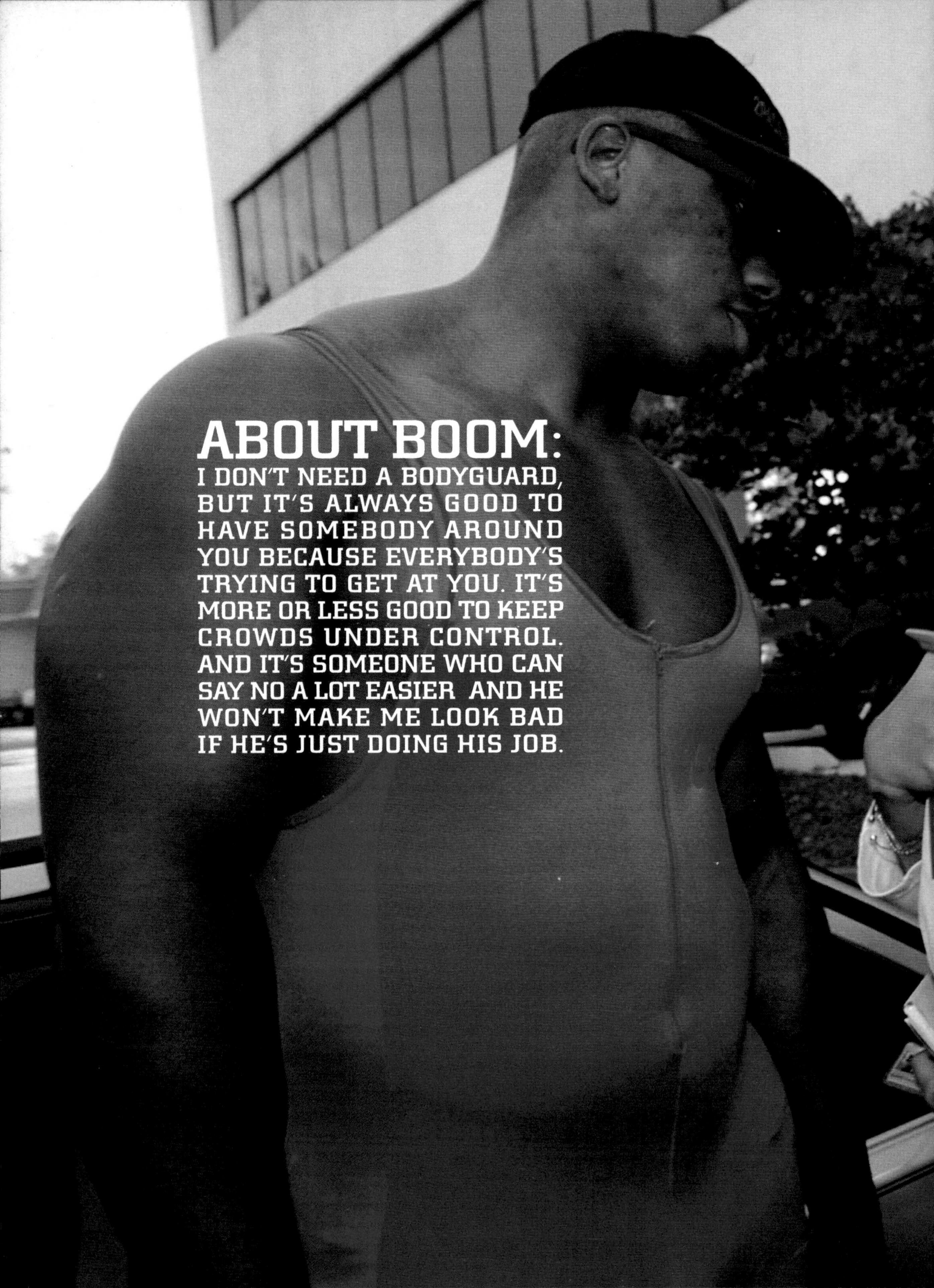

ABOUT BOOM:

I DON'T NEED A BODYGUARD, BUT IT'S ALWAYS GOOD TO HAVE SOMEBODY AROUND YOU BECAUSE EVERYBODY'S TRYING TO GET AT YOU. IT'S MORE OR LESS GOOD TO KEEP CROWDS UNDER CONTROL. AND IT'S SOMEONE WHO CAN SAY NO A LOT EASIER AND HE WON'T MAKE ME LOOK BAD IF HE'S JUST DOING HIS JOB.

adidas

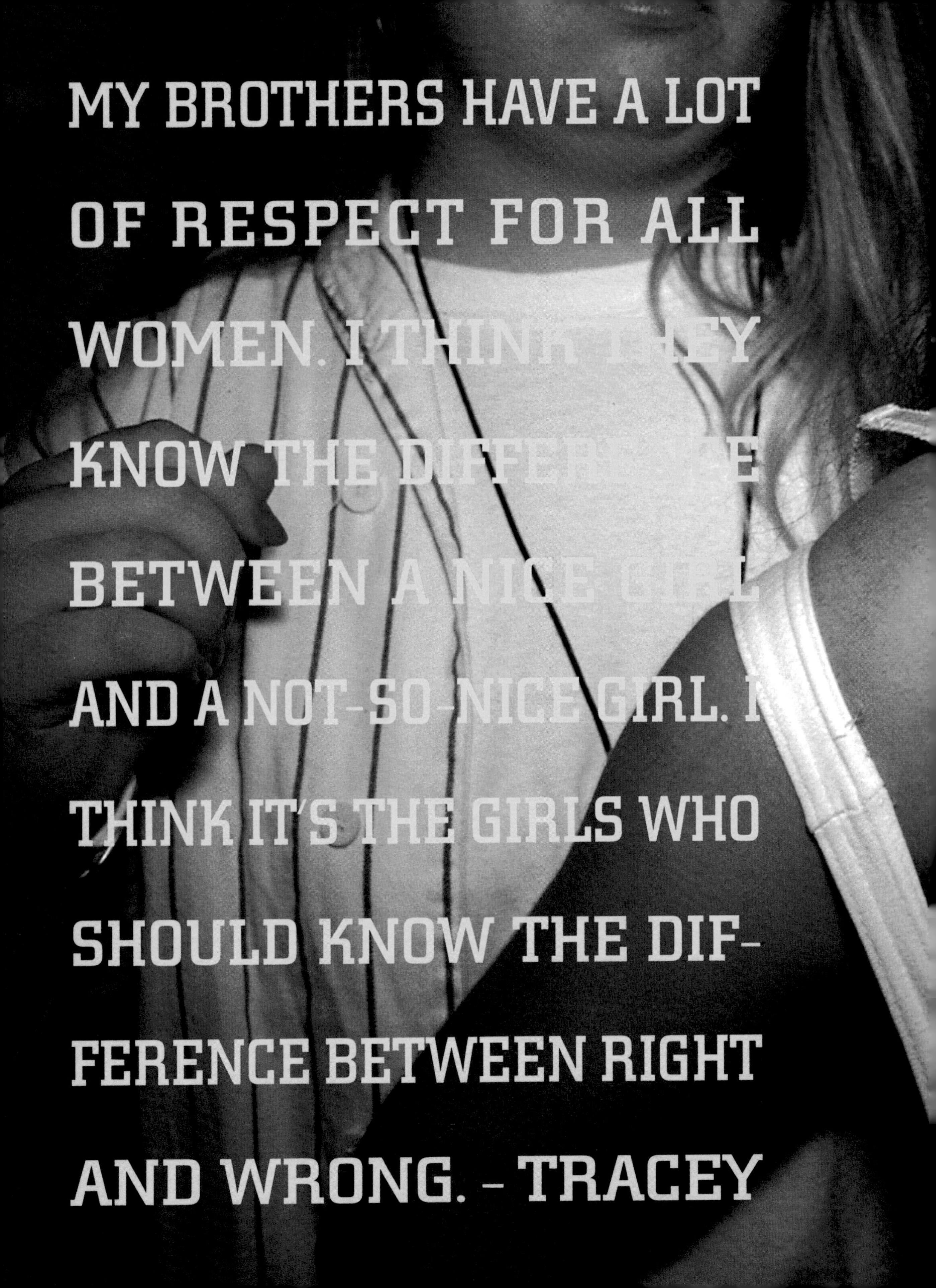

MY BROTHERS HAVE A LOT OF RESPECT FOR ALL WOMEN. I THINK THEY KNOW THE DIFFERENCE BETWEEN A NICE GIRL AND A NOT-SO-NICE GIRL. I THINK IT'S THE GIRLS WHO SHOULD KNOW THE DIFFERENCE BETWEEN RIGHT AND WRONG. – TRACEY

Donnie used to get all the girls cuz he had the money. We got a lot of karma with

girls. We generally like the same girls, but we never chase the same ones.

ONE TIME WE WERE HAVING A FIGHT AND I WAS HOLDING HIM BY THE SHIRT UP NEAR HIS NECK AND HE WAS JUST PUNCHING AWAY AT ME. I WAS TRYING NOT TO PUNCH HIM BACK. I DON'T KNOW WHY THIS PARTICULAR TIME I WOULDN'T PUNCH HIM BECAUSE WE'D PUNCHED EACH OTHER BEFORE, WE'D HAD CRAZY FIGHTS BEFORE. HE WAS JUST SWINGING AWAY, PUNCHING ME ABOUT A HUNDRED TIMES IN ONE MINUTE. FINALLY I GOT FED UP AND PUNCHED HIM IN THE FACE. RIGHT WHEN I HIT HIM, MY FATHER WALKED IN THE DOOR AND KICKED MY ASS! – DONNIE

13
BOSTON
ALL ACCESS
ST. BOSTON
CAMBRIDGE
ST. PROVIDENCE

DID DONNIE GIVE YOU THE NAME "MARKY MARK"? NO. I KNOW HE SAYS HE DID... WELL...IT'S UP IN THE AIR. **BUT YOU FEEL IT'S YOUR NAME...** OF COURSE IT'S MY NAME. I'M THE ONLY MOTHERFUCKER WHO ANSWERS TO IT. THE ONLY MOTHERFUCKER GETTIN' PAID FROM THAT NAME.

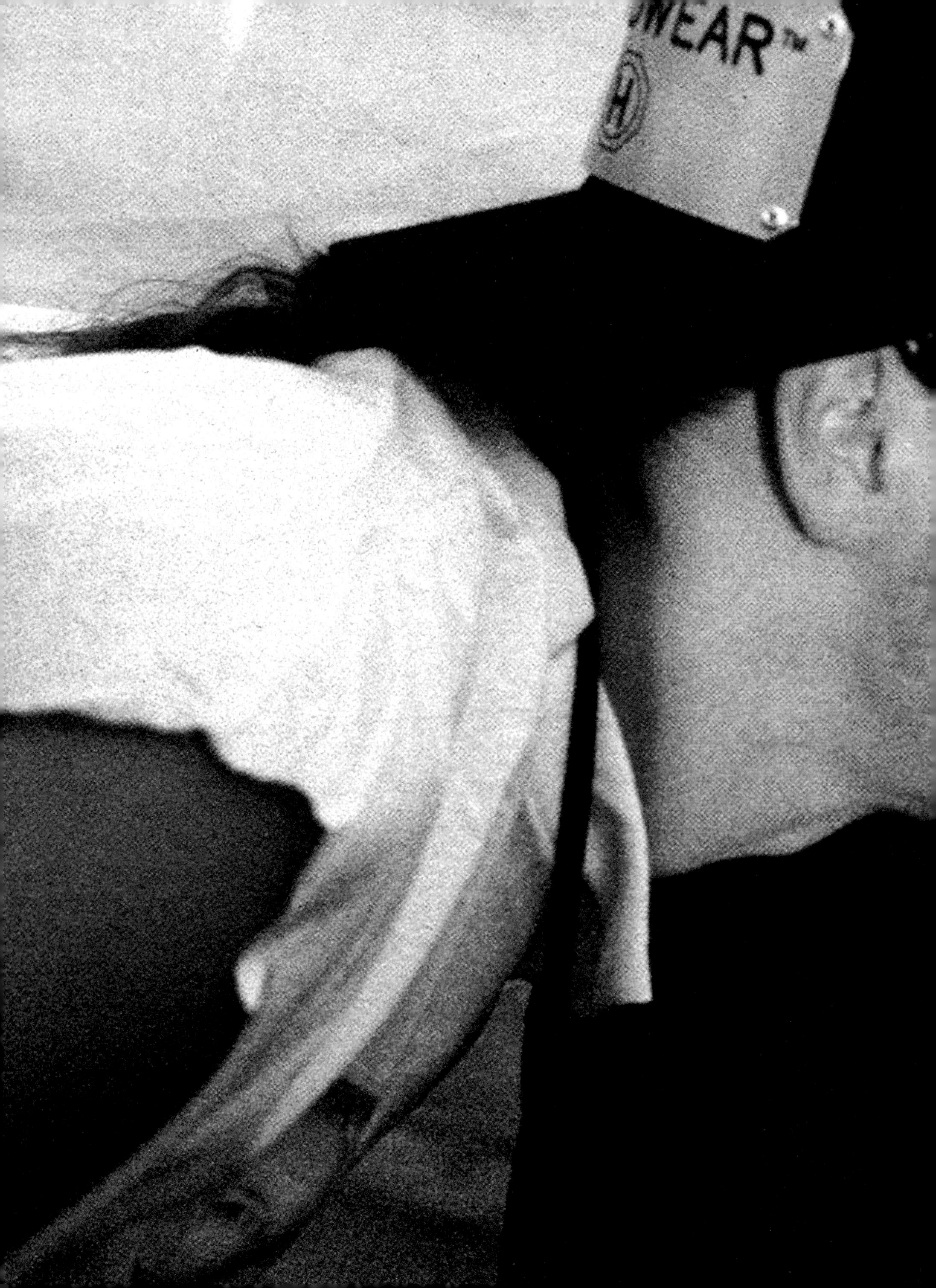
WEAR™

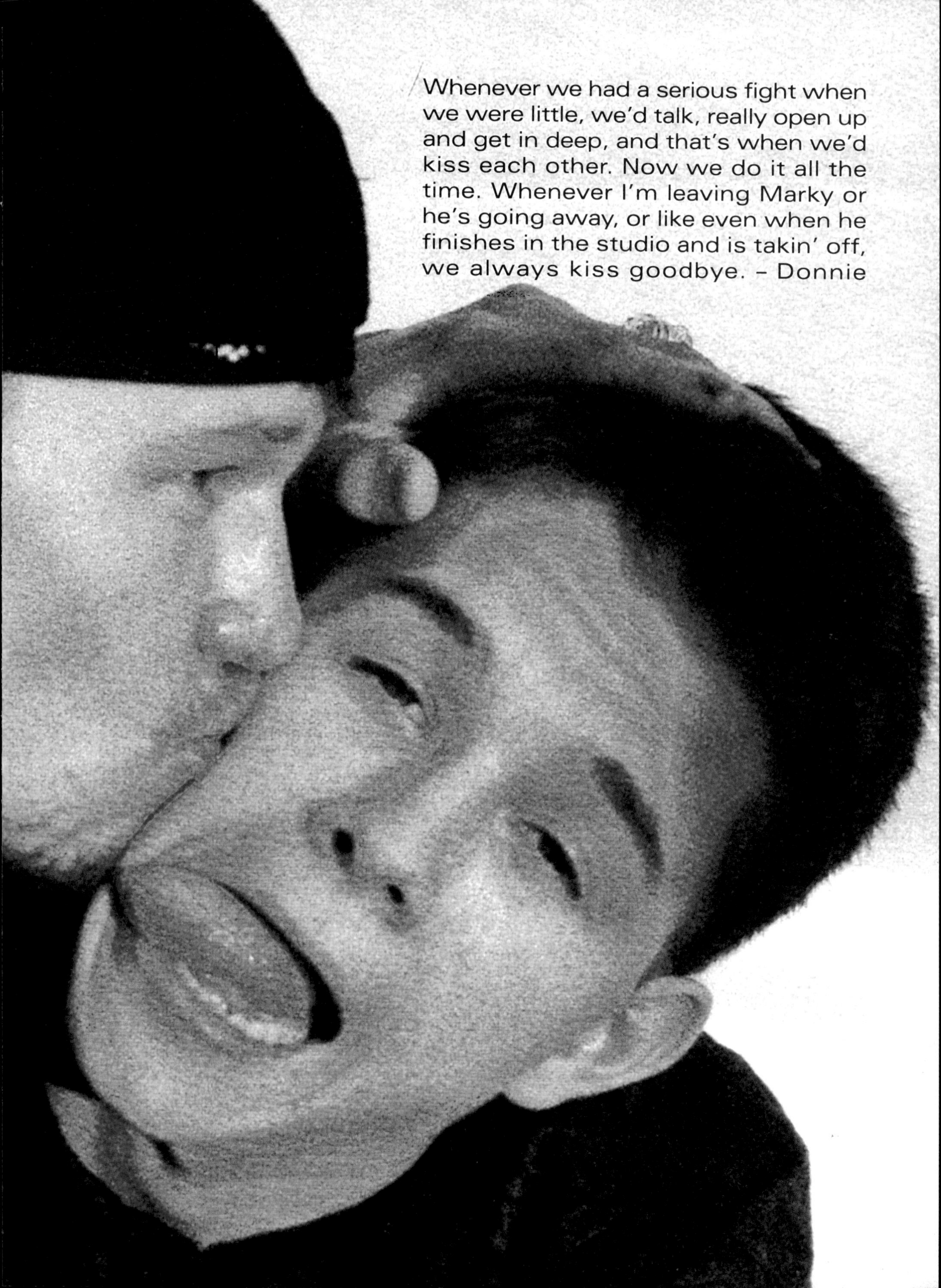

Whenever we had a serious fight when we were little, we'd talk, really open up and get in deep, and that's when we'd kiss each other. Now we do it all the time. Whenever I'm leaving Marky or he's going away, or like even when he finishes in the studio and is takin' off, we always kiss goodbye. – Donnie

ME AND DONNIE HAVEN'T HAD A FIGHT IN A LONG TIME, A REAL GOIN'-AT-IT,

DUKE -'EM-UP FIGHT. BUT I FEEL, YES, I 'WILL' WAX THAT ASS IF I HAVE TO.

MONEY IS GOING TO MAKE MY POCKETS FATTER. IT'S GOING TO MAKE PEOPLE LOOK AT ME DIFFERENTLY. IT'S GOING TO MAKE ME LIVE A LITTLE BIT MORE COMFORTABLY.

HONDA
adidas
DR
100

I worked my fuckin' ass off this year. I'm staying out of trouble. I don't have to worry about get-tin' locked up or get-tin' into no dumb shit.

TELL ME ABOUT THAT TATTOO. IT'S SYLVESTER THE CAT WITH TWEETY BIRD IN HIS MOUTH. HOW'D YOU GET IT? I WENT TO THE TATTOO STORE AND SAID 'GIVE ME THAT TATTOO!' WELL, WHY'D YOU PICK TWEETY BIRD AND THE CAT? I ONLY PICKED IT BECAUSE I WANTED TO COVER UP WHAT WAS THERE BEFORE. WHAT WAS THERE BEFORE? A PLAYING CARD, A CLUB. I DID IT ON MY OWN. I MADE THE CLUB OUT OF INDIA INK. HOW WOULD YOU DESCRIBE THE SYLVESTER AND TWEETY TATTOO? IT'S CORNY. I REGRET GETTING IT BECAUSE IT MARKS UP MY BODY FOR LIFE. AND IF I EVER DO ANYTHING BAD THEY CAN IDENTIFY ME BY IT.

MARK ON HIS THIRD NIPPLE:

IT'S COOL, IT'S UNIQUE. NOT TOO MANY PEOPLE HAVE THEM, AND IT'S NOT HAZARDOUS TO MY HEALTH OR ANYTHING. IT'S NOT SOMETHING TO BE ASHAMED ABOUT. IT'S DOPE. AND BITCHES LIKE TO SUCK IT.

Calvin Klein

I don't like posing bec

ause it's very unnatural.

How do you feel about older women and gay men all wanting you?
I think it's an honor. You know, gay men are not my preference so I'm not as excited as I am about the older women part of it, but people have their likes and dislikes and I respect everybody for that and if I make people happy and entertain them, then cool. But I don't suck dick.

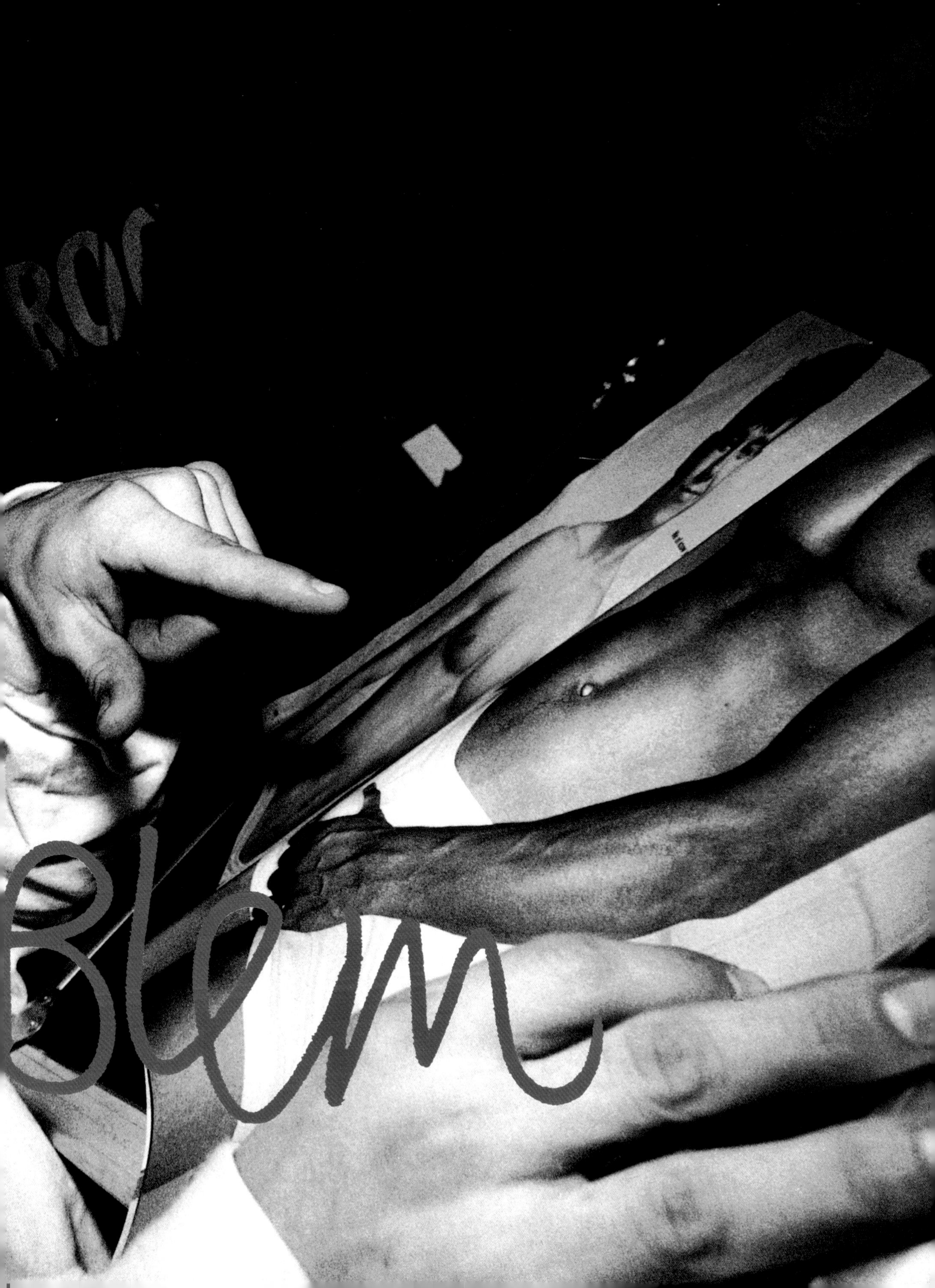
Blem

I'VE REALLY BEEN GROWING UP. I'M IN THE AIDS GENERATION. FOR THE PAST FOUR YEARS I'VE BEEN HEARING NOTHING BUT "SAFE SEX" AND THESE PAST FOUR YEARS HAVE BEEN MY STRONG SEX YEARS. SO, YEAH,

I'VE BEEN SAFE, DEFINITELY, FOR THE MOST PART. MY FIRST GIRL, WE DID IT WITH-OUT A CONDOM ONCE... TWICE. SHE WAS A VIR-GIN TOO. OUT OF ALL MY FRIENDS, I'M THE ONLY ONE WHO DOESN'T HAVE A BABY.

I'M NOT LOOKING

for a girl to throw herself at me. That's not the woman that I want to spend my life with. There has to be mutual respect, mutual love, mutual feelings. And the girl...I would have to be as quick to throw myself at her feet as she at mine.

OTRE
DAM

There's only going to be so much tits and ass coming his way before he realizes that he wants a brain. – Donnie

I think that the fans see

him as a sex sym

Chippendale's type of dude and a great performer. I look at Mark as a friend, because we were there, I was there, before the record came out and during the process of everything happening and before all the big fame and stuff happened. I know what kind of person he is. So we just look at each other as being friends. We don't look at each other as being famous, and I think we never will. – DJ Terry

Maryland Club

SLAM DUNK

WHEN YOU STARTED PLAYING BASKETBALL YOU WERE PRETTY SMALL. WERE OTHER PEOPLE BIGGER THAN YOU? OTHER PEOPLE ARE STILL BIGGER THAN ME.

One of the family jokes is that when Mark was about three he would get in front of anything where he could see his reflection. It could be the toaster or the oven and he would climb up on top of the counter and sit in front of us and

POSE

you know, trying to flex his muscles when all there was was little bones. – Alma

When people say he has a great body, the only thing they're doing is telling the truth. He has a great physique. I know people who've worked out twice as long as him and don't look that good. – Donnie

HE WAS TRYING TO GET ME TO WORK OUT WITH HIM, AND HE ALWAYS TELLS ME, "I USE REVERSE PSYCHOLOGY, MA." AND HE CAME IN ONE DAY AND SAID, "I THINK I'LL JOIN YOU UP AT THE SENIOR CITIZENS' WORKOUT CLUB." AND I SAID, "WHAT DO YOU MEAN! I'M NOT OLD!" SO HE SAID, "WELL, I DON'T KNOW IF YOU COULD DO THE REGULAR GYM, BUT..." AND I SAID, "YES I COULD!" AND I ENDED UP JOINING! AND HATED EVERY MINUTE OF IT! BUT HE WAS SO PROUD OF ME THAT I JOINED. I REALLY RESPECT HIM FOR WORKING OUT. IT'S A LOT OF WORK AND YOU NEED TO BE DEDICATED TO IT; DAYS YOU DON'T WANT TO GO, YOU HAVE TO GO. – ALMA

Protilla

Hot Stuff (protein powder)
Metabalol (laurel powder)
frozen strawberries
pineapple juice

Blend in electric blender.

Drink!

IS

very

rare

Has Mark changed very much since you've known him?

OH YEAH.

He became big so quick that he had to change. He had to grow up. A lot of people were telling him things, instilling things in his head. He's definitely learned a lot since the beginning of all this. – Hector

I KNOW
he's like me, he don't want nobody to tell him nothing. Sometimes I refrain from telling him what I think he should do because I know he doesn't want to hear it just like I didn't want to hear it, you know what I'm saying? - Donnie

WHEN I FIRST HEARD HE DROPPED HIS PANTS I ASKED, "WHY DO YOU HAVE TO DO THAT

TO HOLD THEM UP. BUT I KNEW THAT EVEN WHEN HE DID IT HE HAD RUNNING

I OFFERED HIM SUSPENDERS AND BELTS AND WHATEVER IT WOULD TAKE
SHORTS ON UNDER THE UNDERWEAR SO IT WASN'T TOO, TOO UPSETTING TO ME.—ALMA

I dropped outta high school

because I thought I had better

things to do, like hanging out

on the corner.

You can motherfuckin' snake and connive any shit you want in life if you got education. Then you know how to use that shit to your advantage and trick motherfuckers and shit, you be the man.

MY 21ST BIRTHDAY: IT WAS

HYPE!

WE HAD SOME BREWS. FIRST TIME I'D HAD A LEGAL BREW, BUT I DIDN'T GET DRUNK. WE WAS JUST CHILLIN'. IT WAS COOL. WHAT DO YOU WANT ME TO SAY?

I'M 21!

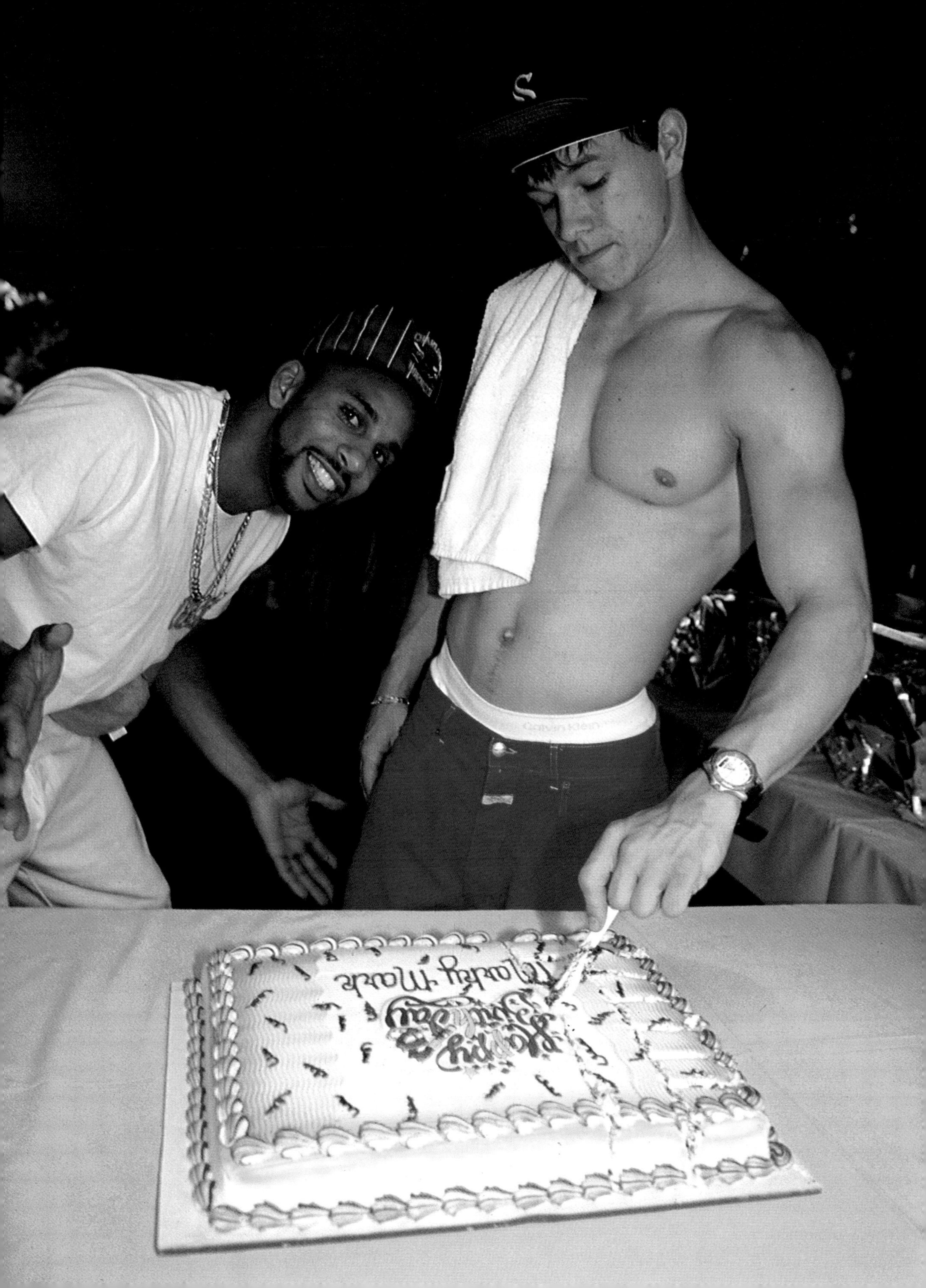

Calvin Klein
Marky Mark

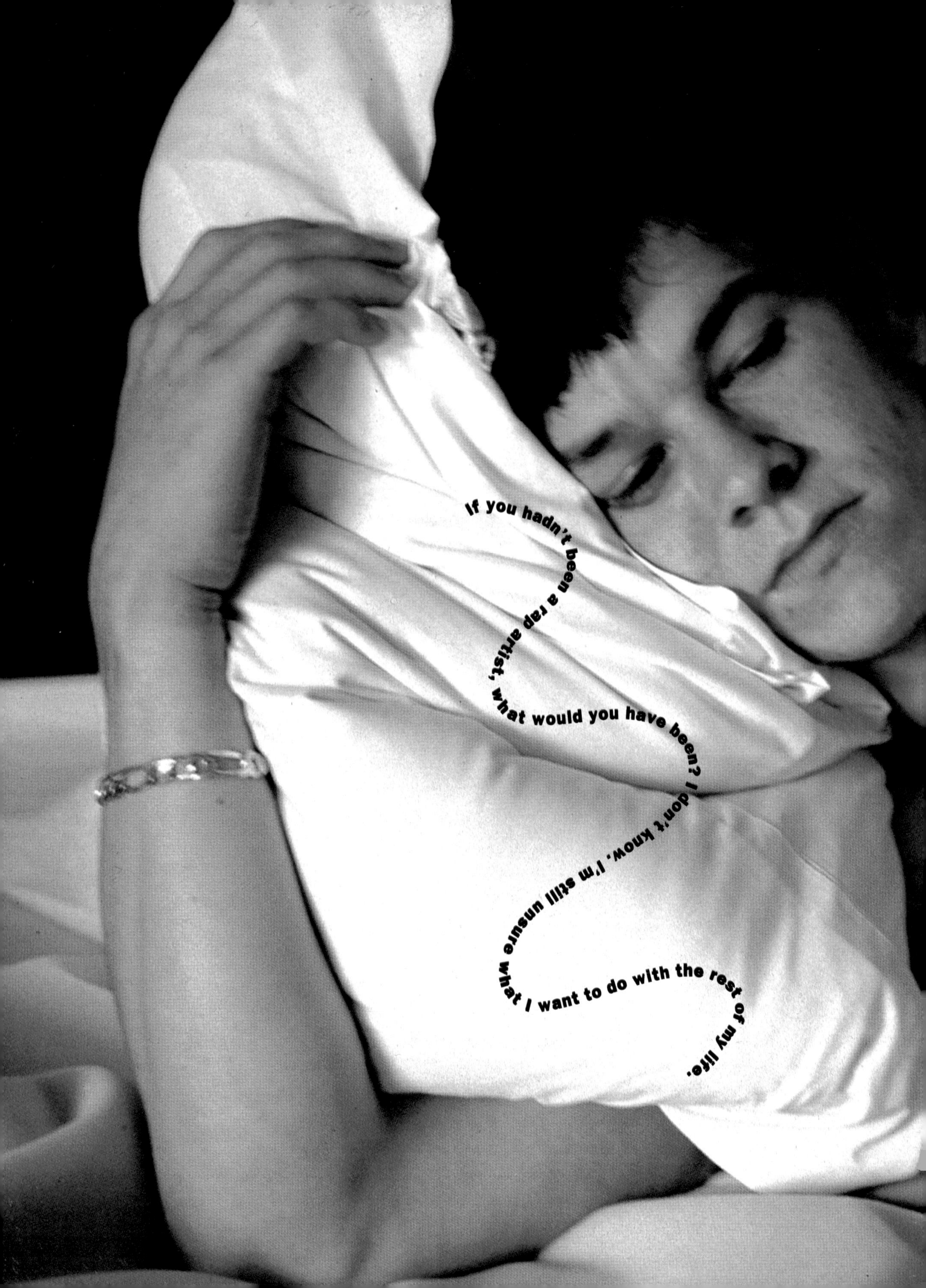
If you hadn't been a rap artist, what would you have been? I don't know. I'm still unsure what I want to do with the rest of my life.

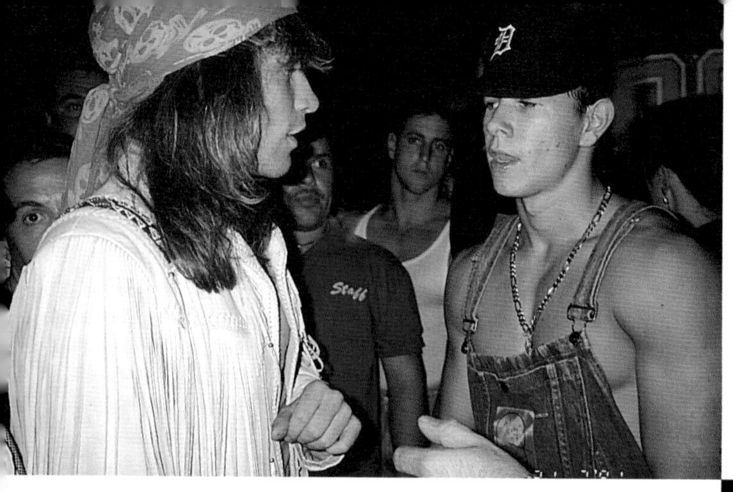

BIG DADDY KANE

COREY BLAKELY
(PERFECT GENTLEMEN)

CHARLOTTE LEWIS

LUKE PERRY

FLEA (RED HOT CHILI PEPPERS)

SF

FLAV IS THE COOLEST motherfucker I know. When you see him perform you think that he's just bugged, but he's really one of the most intelligent people I know. He's very down to earth, very outgoing, he cares. He shows his feelings towards people a lot easier than most would and he does it in a caring way. Basically he's just the coolest motherfucker I know.

CHEESE

is the man. He's the all-around man. You know, Flav and everybody is chill, but Cheese is the man. It's like when we started on the record, we went into the studio together. I could say a million good things about him but to sum it up, he's been the inspiration in my career. He has really helped me and taught me a lot of things about business and just about life. Him being out on his own for a few years kind of separated us, but doing this has really brought us back together and tighter than we've ever been. We were tight when we were little, but all we were doing was fighting with each other anyway. Now we're accomplishing things together and it's really made our parents very proud.

We've both gone through a lot in different ways. He's got 21 years under his belt, and he didn't walk around with his eyes closed. I'm 23 and I didn't walk around with my eyes closed either. We've gone through different but similar things. It's not like we've been worlds apart but we have experienced different things.

I don't feel that he's any more or less of a man than me. – Donnie

adidas

HE DOESN'T forget where he came from. He remembers his friends. Mark feels bad that some of his friends are still on the street. He'd like to see good things happen for them. Every once in a while he'll take one of them out on the road, to give them a chance to see that there's more out there than hanging on the street. – Alma

I'M VERY HAPPY

that Donnie chose to do what he did for Mark. Even if nothing else came out of it, just for the relationship that they have gotten out of it. It's proven that family will do anything for family. I'm very happy about that part of it all. – Tracey

MARKY MARK

Mark and I had an argument, and both of us, just out of our stubbornness in not wanting to give in, didn't talk. I thought about it, and realized that your family's so important and that you don't have to be stubborn and your pride doesn't have to get in the way of your relationship. The end result was instead of holding out as I normally would have done, I apologized, and as I was apologizing, he was apologizing to me for not being able to say he was sorry first. – Tracey

SPIRIT OF

It's home.
Boston
is home.

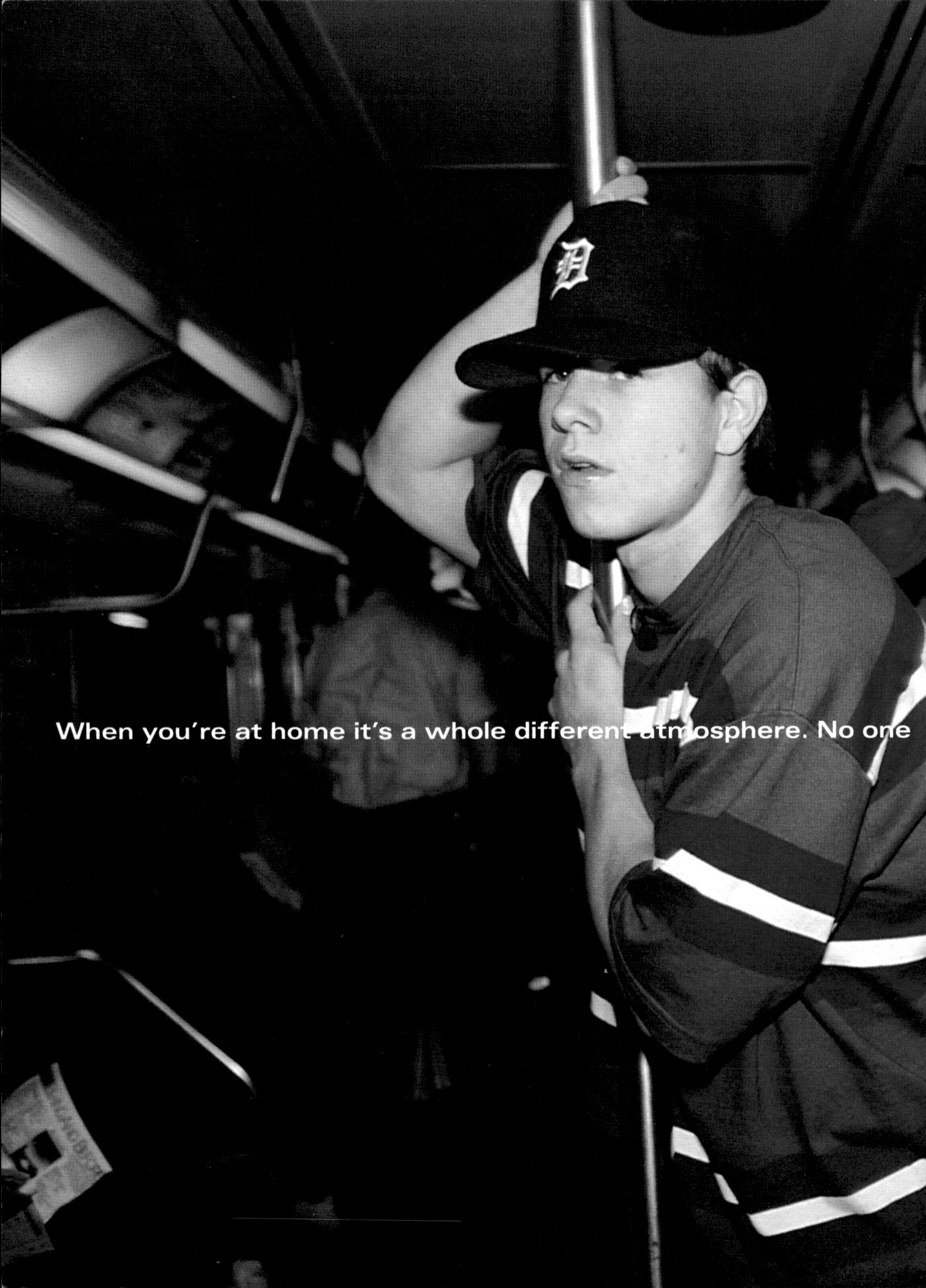
When you're at home it's a whole different atmosphere. No one

is really expecting to see you, so no one is really looking for you.

Directley After Find out About fiances OPP scandle

yea Booms in the House

Mega leany'o Based out

Spec. F.X.

The Dick from the Black Crowes

To much ritlen!

Leatherfa

To gettin Raped

Them Crab iEh

Portaying An image

DICK SCOTT: THAT'S THE MAN

IN MY

M-LOU: THE BIG INSPIRATION

CAREER

THANK YOU

Mark does not want anyone to feel left out, so he thanks everybody. Lynn thanks:

Alma Conroy,

Tracey Wahlberg,

Dick Scott,

Miguel Melendez,

Lenny L. Lewin,

Interscope -

Jimmy Iovine,

Chuck Reed,

Lori Earl.

Polaroid -

Kent Buschle,

Greg Venne.

Ilana Haiken,

Rachel Ruderman,

Mamiya - H. Froehlich.

Bruno Nesci,

Maddy Miller,

Clone-A-Chrome